The Fight of My Life

By Thomas Beavers

Copyright © 2017 Thomas Beavers
All rights reserved. No part of this book may be reproduced or transmitted in any form or by any means without written permission from the author.

ISBN: 978-1-938950-77-3

Greater is He Publishing
9824 E. Washington St.
Chagrin Falls Ohio 44023
P O. Box 46115
Bedford Ohio, 44146

Contents

CHAPTER 1	13
CHAPTER 2	19
CHAPTER 3	27
CHAPTER 4	33
CHAPTER 5	43
CHAPTER 6	57
CHAPTER 7	71
CHAPTER 8	83
CHAPTER 9	93
CHAPTER 10	103

Introduction:

THE FIGHTS OF MY LIFE

It was Oprah Winfrey, when playing Sofia on *The Color Purple,* who said, "All my life, I had to fight!" I can definitely concur with this statement. Although I grew up in a single parent home, my mother has been a judge since the days of my youth. I don't profess to have grown up in the streets. I don't profess to have seen days where utilities got cut off. I don't profess to have grown up in poverty. Still, in spite of it all, I've had my fair share of fights.

My first fight was the relationship with my father. My parents divorced when I was five years old. I saw my dad until I was seven and didn't see him again until I was fourteen years old. I didn't know if he was dead or alive. I remember staying home watching the Ricky Lake Talk Show. I'd watch other families who'd been separated get reunited and would lay in my bed and cry because I longed to be reunited with my father. I never resented my father for not being there; I just didn't understand. All of my other friends had fathers to come to their games except for me. Even when we reunited after being separated for seven years, the relationship was off and on.

Things are totally different now. I see my dad at least once per week. I can count on one hand the number of sports games he showed up to when I was a child, but now he's at church listening to me preach every Sunday. My dad is saved. My dad is redeemed. My dad is a new creature in Christ, and we now have a consistent, vibrant, and growing relationship. I understand my dad. He was absent not because he didn't love me. Rather, he was absent because he was in the fight of his life and didn't know how to win. He coped, but his methods of coping took him away from his children. That fight has now been won. Our relationship is not perfect, but it's a thousand times better than it was. I love my dad, and I know that he loves me.

My second fight was to be a father. My mother remarried after she and my biological father divorced. I must admit that I felt "some type of way." Even though my biological dad was absent at the time, I didn't want anyone to take his place. My new dad didn't have a chance. No love from a father was better than some love from him; at least that's what I thought.

I remember telling him, "You ain't my daddy!" I had no clue then, that I'd soon marry a woman who already had children. In some instances, my children would feel about me the same way that I felt about the man my mother married after my father. I too would one day hear the words, "You ain't my daddy!"

When raising children, I now know to show attention, authority, and affirmation, in that order. I didn't know that when I first got married. I'd show authority with no attention. I'd give discipline without having established a relationship. Although I know what to do concerning my children, I'm still learning how to do it. God is gracing me for this journey as a father, and my children are giving me grace as well. If I'm honest, I'm still in this fight. I don't always do or say the right things as a parent. I haven't reached perfection, but I'm striving every day. Sometimes, winning the fight is not necessarily getting to where you want to be. Rather, it's refusing to settle for where you are. By not settling for where you are, you actively take steps to get to where you want to be. Sometimes, victory is not in the destination. Victory is sometimes in what we learn during the journey.

My third fight was for my marriage. You're saying, "He's a pastor. Doesn't he know that marriage comes before children?" You are right. I do know this. I'm no better than those who didn't, but I did get married before I had children. I placed the fights in this order to keep the father themes congruent.

However, I've had to fight for my marriage. Marriage is a joy, but every day is a learning curve. I can't seem to ever have this thing totally figured out.

On top of getting married at twenty-two years of age, I married into a blended family. My wife already had children. We met during my senior year at Kentucky State University. She was in graduate school. I had never been totally on my own. She was. I was still dependent on my parents. She wasn't. I really didn't know what I was getting myself into. At the same time, I had no fear. I didn't sweat or get nervous on my wedding day. I had total peace that God was with me. I wasn't scared, but everyone else was scared for me—rightfully so. I couldn't take care of myself, and I surely couldn't take care of a woman and three children. Years later, I have the joy of knowing that my wife didn't marry me for stuff. I didn't have anything. She saw potential in me, and took a chance.

Eventually, we moved back to Birmingham, Alabama, and my wife from Cincinnati, Ohio had to adapt to the south. She was actively involved in a church that she loved in Lexington, Kentucky, but now she had to adapt to New Rising Star Church. As great as New Rising Star was, it wasn't what she was used to. To make matters worse, I couldn't move and go to Cincinnati. My call is not just to preach; it's a world-wide call with Birmingham as its base. When I put myself in her shoes, I realize it would be really hard for me too. She moved to an unfamiliar place for me, which wouldn't be as easy for me to do for her. Amongst the struggles we were having at home, adjusting to a church she didn't have the option of choosing made it more difficult. Without ever talking to my grandfather, the current pastor, God told me to come home, sit at his feet, and I would one day be the pastor. The church wasn't perfect, but it was a great church. She just wanted a choice.

We tried to keep it together, but things eventually fell apart; or maybe they fell into place. We experienced both a public separation and a public reconciliation. We are not where we are going to be, but we are one thousand times farther than where we used to be. My victory is not yet in the destination. It's in the lessons I'm learning along the way.

My fifth fight was as a pastor. After succeeding my grandfather in May 2010, he and I were immediately posted on www.pimppreachers.com. We were compared to the likes of Joel Osteen and his father, Matthew Hagee and his father, Franklin Graham and his father, Kenneth Price and his father, and many others. This comparison was not in a good way. Instead, it was highlighting the practice of nepotism in the church, when pastors pass the church to their corrupt and unqualified sons or their corrupt and unqualified family bloodline. I did succeed my grandfather; however, it was anything but nepotism. The author of the article highlighted that I was unlearned, not knowing that I was in school at the time working on a doctoral degree. Aside from this, the author didn't know that degrees don't qualify you for ministry. Only God can do that. As bad as I wanted to speak out, I couldn't. My words would only add fuel to the fire. God did give me the last laugh. I used the article in one of the chapters of my doctoral dissertation. God allowed my enemies to work on my behalf.

My fights were not only outside the church; they were also inside the church. God blessed our church to have a smooth transition, but it wasn't a normal transition. There was no congregational vote. God spoke to Dr. Tommy Chappell, and he appointed me as the pastor. He prepared our leadership two years before he ever acted on this decision. Despite the preparation, some people had feelings about how the transition was made that were initially suppressed but eventually came out later.

On top of this, New Rising Star was very successful under the leadership of my grandfather; the church went from forty-three members to fifteen hundred, to establishing a day care center, credit union, and community support corporation, to building our family life center with three million dollars cash, and much more. When I became the pastor, many people were complacent because of previous success. What do you do when your church is successful but still tasked with the challenge of serving "This Present Age?" My grandfather retired. Many people who worked for him stayed in positions, paid and unpaid, but were tired as well. Some were loyal to him but not loyal to me. Nevertheless, God tasked me to lead these people: those who wanted me and those who didn't; those who were on board and those who weren't; those who were in drive and those who were in reverse, park, and neutral.

Things were great until we changed our methods of accomplishing the same tasks that we had been doing for years: sharing Christ via evangelism, encountering Christ via worship, connecting with people via fellowship, growing in Christ via discipleship, and serving the world via ministry. When we changed methods, it afflicted the comfortable and comforted the afflicted. Powers that be started to rise up until I eventually had to deal with some things head on. By God's grace, the church is not torn up, the ship is not turned over, and we are moving forward.

My sixth fight was as a community leader. The Lord Jesus has placed a grace on our ministry to empower our community through education, financial literacy, workforce development, housing, recreation, and the church. I messed around and told the city that we would start a charter school to give children more options. I also told the city that we would buy a vacant mall to expand our community efforts. We were immediately on everyone's radar. Some people love the vision, and some people don't. The charter school was approved, but the mall is still in progress.

I was afraid to tell my dream to New Rising Star Church and to the city of Birmingham, Alabama. I have a dream to bless the city and beyond, but my primary responsibility is the church I serve. How do I pursue the dream without neglecting the church? How do I engage and shepherd the church without neglecting the dream? As kids, we are told to dream big. When I started really dreaming big, the same people started to tell me that the dream was impossible and that the dream was too big. Is my dream too big, or is their vision too small? I don't know how the dream is going to come to pass. However, I do know that it will come to pass. My focus isn't the "how." It's the "who." God's hand will certainly fulfill what his mouth has spoken (1Kg.8:15).

On top of outsiders telling me that my dream was too big, there were also internal fights. People attached themselves to me and to the vision that God gave me, but I didn't realize they had ulterior motives of personal gain. Once, when I was preaching at another church, they pinned a corsage on my suit. The corsage represented "beauty." I was afraid while they were pinning it on me because I didn't want them to stick me with the needle in the process. Thankfully, the corsage sat beautifully on my suit without me getting stuck. God then spoke to me about a situation that took place concerning some people that were close friends. He said:

"There are people who attached themselves to you and the vision that I've given you under the auspices of bringing things together and making things beautiful; however, these people had ulterior motives. As a result, they didn't make things beautiful. Instead,

they stuck you, leaving you in the fight of your life. Don't be fooled, Thomas. The fight of your life is not the people who stuck you. It's the internal war in your heart to forgive the people who stuck you. You must forgive. I will heal you and deal with those who've stuck you and caused you to hurt."

Between where you are and the place you want to be is tension. The fight of your life is located in the tension. The question is, "How do I navigate this tension?" I am not an expert. I'm still learning myself. At the same time, there are some biblical pragmatic principles that have equipped me for victory. I believe that these same principles will equip you for victory. If you feel like you are in the fight of your life, this read is for you. Enjoy, Engage, but most of all, Execute! You are now reading, *The Fight Of My Life*.

It's Time to Throw Hands

- What is the most pressing fight of my life?
- Where do I sense God taking me or doing in my life in the next 5-10 years?
- Could this Fight be necessary to develop me for my future? If so in what ways?

-Prayer:

Lord, as hard as my fight is/was, I thank you. Thank you that even when I don't understand, you have a greater purpose and a greater plan. Thank you Jesus for using my present fights to prepare me for my future, in Jesus' name, AMEN!

CHAPTER 1
You Don't Have to Hide Your Fight

Perhaps as you are reading this, you feel like a boxer who's in the fight of his or her life. Maybe your fight is a broken marriage that you're believing God to put back together. Maybe your fight is a wayward child that you're believing God to change and send back home. Maybe your fight is a sickness in your body that doctors have little to no hope of curing. Maybe your fight is poverty, unemployment, or something else. Whatever it is, it's a real fight that often leaves you emotionally constipated. Have you ever been in a place where you were crying in your heart but tears wouldn't come out of your eyes?

What's even worse is that many of us mask our fight as if nothing is wrong. We carry on as if our lives are perfectly intact. We are public and social media successes but at the same time private failures. Why do we do this? Satan grips us with shame and embarrassment. We don't want the word to get out about our fight because we don't want to run the risk of people thinking less of us. Satan uses the fear that we have of being shamed and embarrassed to further isolate us. We start to feel like we are the only ones going through what we are going through when that is just not true. Scripture teaches us, "The temptations in your life are no different from what others experience. But God is faithful. He will not allow the temptation to be more than you can stand. When you are tempted, he will show you a way out so that you can endure" (1Cor.10:13). When you are in the fight of your life, remember this:

1. You are not the first to fight this battle, and you won't be the last.
2. God is faithful, even when you are unfaithful.
3. God knows how much you can handle without breaking, and he has measured out your fight not to exceed your capacity.
4. God always provides an exit out of your fight.

God wants to free you from the shame and embarrassment of your fight. With public failure, there is always public deliverance. "And they have defeated him by the blood of the Lamb and by their testimony. And they did not love their lives so much that they were afraid to die" (Rev.12:11). The blood of the lamb, Jesus the Christ, has already been shed. The only thing left is for you to share your testimony. It sounds cliché, but it's so true; you will never have a testimony without a test. Your testimony of real brokenness experienced from a real fight gives others encouragement that they too can have victory in their fights. Your fight is not for you. It's for others who will face the same fight after you. Perhaps this is why Jesus said to Peter, "When you are converted, reach back and strengthen your brothers" (Lk.22:32).

This is the very reason that I'm writing this book. It was A.W. Tozer who once said, "Before God uses a man greatly, he hurts him severely." I could easily write about all of my successes: being a straight "A" student in high school, accepting my calling into the ministry at the age of eighteen and preaching my first sermon on July 16, 2000, lettering in basketball four years at Kentucky State University, serving as Mr. Kentucky State University on student government in college, graduating Magna Cum Laude with a B.S. in Biology, obtaining an Master of Divinity and Doctor of Ministry from Beeson Divinity School of Samford University of Birmingham, Alabama, and much more. However, there is something about brokenness and real transparency that makes one a whole lot more relatable to people. Therefore, this book is about how God used my brokenness (marrying a wonderful woman who already had three children and bringing her back home to a traditional Baptist church where we almost fell apart, raising kids on a WIC program and other government assistance until we could do better, witnessing my wife deliver a still born child, being betrayed by close friends who attached themselves to my God-given vision for their own personal gain, and much more) to bless people and how he can and will do the same thing for you.

Rather than tell you about my successes, I'd rather tell you about my fights. The apostle Paul did the exact same thing:

That experience is worth boasting about, but I'm not going to do it. I will boast about my weaknesses. If I wanted to boast, I would be no fool in doing so, because I would be telling the truth. But I won't do it, because to give me credit beyond what they can see in my life or hear in my message, even though I have received such wonderful revelations from God. So to keep me from becoming proud, I was given a thorn in my flesh, a messenger from Satan to torment me and keep me from becoming proud. Three different times I begged the Lord to take it away. Each time he said, 'My grace is all you need. My power works best in weakness." So now I am glad to boast about my weaknesses, so that the power of Christ can work through me. That's why I take pleasure in my weaknesses, and in the insults, hardships, and persecutions, and troubles that I suffer for Christ. For when I am weak, then I am strong (2Cor.12:5-10).

It's Time to Throw Hands

- In what ways have I hid my fight?
- Why do I hide my fight?
- Is there anyone in my life with whom I can be transparent without fear of being judged? If so, who in my life can I talk to?
- How often do I reach out to them?

-Prayer:

Lord please send people into to my life with whom I can be transparent. Thank you for separating the real from the fake. I confess that I need you. I also need someone on earth to talk with. Give me discernment as to who I can open up to, in Jesus' name, AMEN!

CHAPTER 2
Recognize the Enemy

Before boxers step into the ring, they spend months training for their opponent. One critical piece of the training process is film. Boxers watch film to recognize their opponent and his or her tactics. As this pertains to a spiritual sense, you must recognize the enemy to win the fight of your life. Ironically, the enemy is not who you think it is. The enemy is not your spouse. The enemy is not your child. The enemy is not your boss. The enemy is not your co-worker. Your enemy is not your condition.

Well, who is my enemy? The enemy is Satan. The biggest trick of Satan is to make people think that he doesn't exist. Satan exists, even though he is rarely seen with the natural eye. Paul teaches us the following:

A final word: Be strong in the Lord and in his mighty power. Put on all of God's armor so that you will be able to stand firm against all strategies of the devil. For we are not fighting against flesh-and-blood enemies, but against evil rulers and against authorities of the unseen world, against mighty powers in this dark world, and against evil spirits in the heavenly places. Therefore, put on every piece of God's armor so you will be able to resist the enemy in the time of evil (Eph.6:10-13).

Paul wrote this discourse at the end of his letter to the church at Ephesus. The book of Ephesians has six chapters. The first three chapters remind us of what God has done for us. God has already blessed us with every spiritual blessing (Eph.1). God has made us alive when we were dead in our trespasses and sins (Eph.2). God both revealed and made available his mysterious plan of salvation to Gentiles and Jews (Eph.3). The last three chapters remind us of how we are to respond to what God has done for us. In other words, the goodness of God demands a response. Our first response is as a Christian. We are to walk worthy of the call of God in all lowliness, meekness, longsuffering, and laboring to keep the unity of the Spirit in the bond of peace (Eph.4:1-Eph.5:21). Our second response is as husband and wife. Husbands are to love wives as Christ loved the church and as their own bodies. Wives are to submit to and respect their husbands (Eph.5:22-33). Our third response is as parent and child. Parents are to raise their children in the ways of the Lord without provoking them to anger, and children are to obey and honor their parents (Eph.6:1-4). Our fourth response is as employee and employer. Employees are to work as unto the Lord, and employers are not to lord their authority over employees (Eph.6:5-9).

After Paul laid out household and family order, he then started talking about spiritual warfare. What does this mean to us? There is a certain order in which our lives must be aligned in response to God's goodness, but it's not going to happen without a fight. Stop getting mad at people, and start getting mad at the real enemy, Satan!

Protect yourself from the schemes of Satan by putting on the whole armor of God.

Then after the battle you will still be standing firm. Stand your ground, putting on the belt of truth and the body armor of God's righteousness. For shoes, put on the peace that comes from the Good News so that you will be fully prepared. In addition to all of these, hold up the shield of faith to stop the fiery arrows of the devil. Put on salvation as your helmet, and take the sword of the Spirit which is the Word of God. Pray in the Spirit at all times and on every occasion. Stay alert and be persistent in your prayers for all believers everywhere (Eph.6:13B-18).

The armor of God stems from the metaphor of a Roman soldier

1. <u>Put on the Belt Of Truth:</u> Roman soldiers had belts around their waists from which all of their other weaponry hung, much like the belt of a police officer. To put on the belt of truth is to center your life around the truth of God and his Word instead of trying to get God to center his life around you. This causes us to win the fight of our lives.

2. <u>Put on the Breastplate Of Righteousness:</u> The breastplate protected the heart. We protect our hearts when we understand the nature of our righteousness. We are righteous, not because of what we've done. We're righteous because of what Jesus did over 2000 years ago through his death on the cross, his burial, and his resurrection. Jesus substituted himself in our place, and he died a death that he did not deserve to pay the debt of sin that we were unable to pay. Through his death, Jesus stripped himself of his righteousness and stripped us of our unrighteousness. He clothed himself in our unrighteousness and clothed us in his righteousness. Because of this, we are made righteous through faith alone in Christ Jesus.

3. <u>Put on the Shoes Of Peace:</u> Roman soldiers had shoes with spikes that kept them from slipping in the heat of battle. Prolonged anger causes one to fall in spiritual

battle. Peace, which comes from our belief and acceptance of the Good News of Jesus' death, burial, and resurrection, causes us to stand.

4. <u>Lift up the Shield Of Faith:</u> Roman soldiers had shields that blocked the darts of the enemy. Satan throws fiery darts of doubt in the heat of spiritual battle. The Shield Of Faith causes us to believe God against all odds, even when it doesn't make sense. Faith is the ability to walk towards a closed door, believing that it will open when we get there. When you approach an automatic door, it's closed upon first sight. Logic says turn around; however, faith says keep walking. The door will open when you get there. Faith causes us to keep moving in a certain direction when logic says turn around. Faith believes God when things don't make sense.

5. <u>Put on the Helmet Of Salvation:</u> A large percentage of spiritual warfare takes place on the battlefield of the mind. Mature believers who win the fight of their lives must master their thought life. Faith alone in Jesus Christ saves us. Once we are saved, our minds must be renewed to think like the Word, not the world.

6. <u>Take the Sword Of The Spirit:</u> The only offensive weapon of the Roman soldier was the sword. The Sword

of the Spirit represents the Word of God. It's impossible to win the fight of your life without the Word of God. Hear the Word, heed the Word, and watch God move on your behalf.

It's Time to Throw Hands

- On the surface, what or whom am I fighting with?
- How is Satan working in this fight?
- Knowing that Satan is my real enemy, does that change how I feel about the person who's become the object of my fight?
- Have I allowed Satan to use me in this fight?
- What should I be praying right now?

-Prayer:

Lord, help me to recognize the enemy in all situations. Please forgive me for the times I've been angry with people when I should have been angry with Satan. Please forgive me for the times I've allowed Satan to use me. I humbly repent, in Jesus' name, AMEN!

CHAPTER 3
Trim the Fat

It's foolish for any boxer to step into the ring without being in shape. Whether the match is three rounds, twelve rounds, or fifteen rounds, the boxer cannot go the distance if his or her stamina is not up to par. Boxers, alongside all athletes, trim fat primarily two different ways: healthy eating and rigorous exercise. The boxer doesn't wait until the night before the fight to change his or her eating habits. The boxer doesn't wait until the night before the fight to start exercising. Boxers eat healthy and put their bodies through strenuous activity long before the fight even starts.

So many people are losing the fight of their lives not because they don't recognize the enemy but because they are spiritually out of shape. We get in shape spiritually by trimming the fat through hearing (eating) the Word and heeding (exercise) the Word. What does your spiritual diet look like? How often are you in the Word of God? Is it once per week when you go to church, or maybe twice per week on Sunday and Wednesday if you attend a mid-week service? Or is it every day? If we feed our physical bodies two to three times per day, seven days per week, how can our souls be nourished and fit for the fight if we are only in the Word once to twice per week, if that?

As stated before, after we hear (eat) the Word, we must heed (exercise) the Word by putting it into practice. Coming to church doesn't fit us for the fight. Applying what we hear inside of the church is what fits us for the fight.

But don't just listen to God's word. You must do what it says. Otherwise, you are only fooling yourselves. For if you listen to the Word and don't obey, it is like glancing at your face in a mirror. You see yourself, walk away, and forget what you look like. But if you look carefully into the perfect law that sets you free, and if you do what it says and don't forget what you heard, then God will bless you for doing it (Jms.1:22-25).

The Word of God is not a mirror for me to see other people's faults and flaws; it's a window for me to see myself. When I hear the Word without heeding the Word, it's like looking at my natural face in a mirror, seeing my flaws, and leaving as if I don't need to fix my face. No person of adequate hygiene would wake up in the morning and put on clothes to go to work without first looking in the bathroom mirror. When we take our first glance into the mirror in the morning, our face needs work. We must wash our face, brush our teeth, comb our hair, and much more before we are ready to start the day. Every time we heed (practice) the Word, we fix the flaws of the human heart and human mind, thus becoming more and more like God.

When we eat too much without exercising, we become physically obese. Many people are spiritually obese. We hear sermon after sermon, tape after tape, visit revival after revival, look at television minister after television minister; but put none of it into practice. We fail to get in shape, creating excess fat in the body of Christ, and we never gain victory in the fight of our lives. I'm tired of singing "Victory Is Mine" without really having the victory. I'm sure that you are too. God has ordained for us to have victory right now, but it requires us to get in shape. Trim the fat by hearing and heeding God's Word.

It's Time to Throw Hands

- How often do I read the Word of God?
- How often do I pray to Jesus?
- Is my prayer and reading time duty based or desire based?
- Do I study for information or transformation?
- Do I practice the Word on purpose?

-Prayer:

Lord, help me to read your Word, that I may know your Word. Most of all, give me the desire to practice your Word in all situations and circumstances, in Jesus' name AMEN!

CHAPTER 4
Other Ways to Trim the Fat?

Aside from hearing (eating) and heeding (exercising) God's Word, we trim the fat by laying aside weight and sin. When was the last time you assessed who was in your life and what was in your life? Is it an asset or a liability? Are they and asset or a liability? Do they add to you or subtract from you? If the thought of a very person drains your spirit, chances are that he or she is a liability and not an asset. If you've ever had a habit that feels good but sets you back at the same time, chances are that it's a liability and not an asset.

What and who do you need to get rid of? What and who do you need to lay aside? This doesn't include marriage and children. These are not relationships that we just lay aside when times get hard. There may be times of separation and even extreme cases of divorce for the sake of peace (1 Cor.7:15), but we are not to throw these relationships away altogether. At the same time, we can't win the fight of our lives carrying things and people that God never intended for us to carry. God never intends for us to carry someone for a lifetime because that person would then become dependent upon us and replace God with us. Sometimes, it's necessary to let people down. It is then and only then that they find themselves at the feet of Jesus.

Soon the house where he was staying was so packed with visitors that there was no more room, even outside the door. While he was preaching God's Word to them, four men arrived carrying a paralyzed man on a mat. They couldn't bring him to Jesus because of the crowd, so they dug a hole through the roof above his head. Then they lowered the man (let him down) on his mat, right down in front of Jesus [at the feet of Jesus] (Mk.2:2-4).

Four friends carried this paralyzed man for a season — not for a lifetime. They knew that if he was going to win the fight of his life and they were going to win the fight of their lives, they couldn't keep doing what they were doing. Knowing that Jesus was their only hope, they brought the man to Jesus. It was so crowded in the house that they couldn't get in; therefore, they climbed on top of the roof (houses in those days had steps that went up to the roof). When they got to the top of the roof, they tore open a hole in the roof and let the paralyzed man down.

The same friends that carried this man for a season are the same friends that let him down. When they let him down, he was at the feet of Jesus, the only one who could heal him and empower him. Have you ever had to let someone down? You went back and forth in your mind. "That's mean of me. I need to save them. I need to help them." This is not always the case. When people become solely dependent upon you, you have not helped them. You have actually hurt them because you have blocked them from seeing, trusting, and depending upon God. Why seek after God when they have you? You've become their god. You can't win the fight of your life carrying people (husband, wife, children, friends, family, etc.) past season. Ask God for wisdom to know when the season is up. Sometimes, we must let people down. They may not like it at first, but at least they'll be at the feet of Jesus. They will thank you later.

Here is another example of trimming the fat, which will help us win the fight of our lives.

Therefore, since we are surrounded by such a huge crowd of witnesses to the life of faith, let us strip off every weight that slows us down, especially the sin that so easily trips us up. And let us run with endurance the race God has set before us. We do this by keeping our eyes on Jesus, the champion who initiates and perfects our faith (Heb.12:1-2).

No runner runs a race with weights attached. Weights are for training, not for the actual test. When the test comes, we must strip off the weight and sin that holds us back. Sometimes, when running and fighting, we get tired and feel like quitting. When we feel like throwing in the towel, we have witnesses in the clouds who catch the towel, encourage us, and throw the towel right back to us. The clouds of witnesses (Heb.12) are found in the hall of faith (Heb.11). These were real people with real issues who conquered their real issues with real faith, and they have now gone on to glory. As they peek over the balcony of Heaven, they witness us in the fight of our lives and encourage us to learn from their stories and testimonies of when they were in the fight of their lives. Their stories provide wisdom and strength for us to assess excess weight in our lives: perhaps a sin, habit, or person. Sometimes, our company perpetuates our sin or ungodly habit. Learning from the stories of these clouds of witnesses gives us strength to assess our lives and remove excess weight accordingly.

Gideon is another example of someone who was in the fight of his life but was able to win by trimming the fat. However, it's important to note that Gideon didn't choose whom to let go of in his life. God made the choice for Gideon. Gideon was in tune with God and obeyed God. The choice was about what was being done, not who was doing it. This means that trimming the fat is never personal. This is why we must allow God to guide us in trimming the fat and not cut people ourselves just because we don't like them. We take things personal, but God is looking at the action. Ask God for wisdom, remain in him, and obey his voice when he speaks. Check this out!

So Jerub-baal (that is, Gideon) and his army got up early and went as far as the spring of Harod. The armies of Midian were camped north of them in the valley near the hill of Moreh. The Lord said to Gideon, "You have too many warriors with you. If I let all of you fight the Midianites, the Israelites will boast to me that they saved themselves by their own strength. Therefore, tell the people, 'Whoever is timid or afraid may leave this mountain and go home.'" So 22,000 of them went home, leaving only 10,000 who were willing to fight. But the Lord told Gideon, "There are still too many! Bring them down to the spring, and I will test them to determine who will go with you and who will not." When Gideon took his warriors down to the water, the Lord told him, "Divide the men into two groups. In one group put all those who cup water in their hands and lap it up with their tongues like dogs. In the other group put all those who kneel down and drink with their mouths in the stream." Only 300 of the men drank from their hands. All the others got down on their knees and drank with their mouths in the stream. The Lord told Gideon, "With these 300 men I will rescue you and give you victory over the Midianites. Send all the others home." (*Judges 7:1-7*)

Gideon teaches us four things about trimming the fat.

1. <u>Everybody you count, you can't count on.</u> Gideon counted 32,000 for battle but could only count on 300 when it was all said and done. Ask yourself two things. How many people can I count inside of my inner circle? How many people inside of my inner circle can I truly count on? An entourage looks wonderful, but what is the use in having a bunch of people around you who look good but make no contribution. Trim the fat.

2. <u>When I'm in the fight of my life, I can't have fearful people inside of my circle.</u> The first group of people that God instructed Gideon to trim was those who were afraid. Gideon went from 32,000 to 10,000. Fear is the opposite of faith. If you have cancer, you don't need someone in your circle who says, "I know someone else who had cancer, and they died." If you are having financial problems, you don't need someone in your circle who says, "I know someone else who had financial problems, and they went bankrupt." If you are having marital issues, you don't need someone in your circle who says, "I know someone else who had

marital problems, and they divorced." If your child is wayward, you don't need someone inside of your circle who says, "I know someone else with a wayward child who never came back home." Trim the fat by getting fearful people out of your circle.

3. <u>When I'm in the fight of my life, I can't have selfish people inside of my circle.</u> God instructed Gideon to take his remaining army to the riverside and let them drink. Those who drank on their knees, putting their face to the water, had to go home. Those who bent their knees, cupped the water, and brought it up to their mouths remained. Gideon went from 10,000 to 300. What was it about the way they drank water? Those who drank from their knees with their face to the water could quench their thirst but couldn't look out for the enemy. Those who drank water by bending their knees and bringing the water to their mouths could quench their thirst and look out for the enemy. Here's the lesson: you don't need people in your circle who fulfill their desires at the expense of your protection. This kind of person is a selfish person. Trim the fat!

4. <u>When I'm in the fight of my life, I must praise God and totally depend on him.</u> When Gideon went to battle with the 300, they didn't have weapons. They only had

trumpets. They didn't lift a finger. They only lifted a sound. Never mistake the power of praise and worship. Praise and worship is your weapon. You don't have to wait until the battle is over to praise God. You must praise God now. Your victory depends on your praise. When Gideon praised God, the enemy was confused and killed himself. Your praise confuses the devil. Your fight has been severe enough for you to have a nervous breakdown, go crazy, lose your mind, stop going to church, leave God, and much more. Satan is confused at how you are still praising God with everything he's thrown your way. Praise God until you see the victory that you already have. Even when people leave whom you thought would always be there, keep praising God! God was waiting to get you to a place where you depend on him only, not people. Trim the fat!

It's Time to Throw Hands

- Who is in my life that I need to get rid of?
- What is in my life that I need to get rid of?
- What fears do I need to get rid of?
- In what areas am I selfish?
- Do I hang around fearful and selfish people?

-Prayer:

Lord Jesus, help me to trim the fat. Show me who I need to get rid of. Show me what I need to get rid of. Give me the strength to trim the fat, no matter how painful it is, in Jesus' name, AMEN!

CHAPTER 5

Who's In Your Corner?

Every boxer must trim the fat before stepping into the ring. However, after they step into the ring, the people in their corner are extremely critical to them winning the fight of their lives. As this pertains to life, so many people do not win the fight of their lives simply because they don't have the right people in their corner.

The person in your corner must be a champion and not a crab. Champions encourage you. Crabs discourage you. You would think that the people in your corner would automatically encourage you. This is not always the case. Sometimes, the one who is supposed to mentor you is the very one who tries to murder you out of a heart of jealousy. It's the typical "crab in a bucket" mentality. As soon as one crab decides to climb out of the bucket (the first in the family to go to college, the first to rise above poverty and make an earnest living, the one who says no to peer pressure, etc.), there is always another crab at the bottom trying to pull it back down. What happens when the very people in your corner (who live in the same house, eat at the same table, go to the same church, go to the same school, work in the same place, etc.), who are supposed to be encouraging you and pushing you to the next level, are the very people who are jealous and trying to bring you down? This is sad but so true in many cases.

An example of this is the classical Saul and David relationship.

When the victorious Israelite army was returning home after David had killed the Philistine, women from all the towns of Israel came out to meet King Saul. They sang and danced for joy with tambourines and cymbals. This was their song: "Saul has killed his thousands, and David his ten thousands!" This made Saul very angry. "What's this?" he said. "They credit David with ten thousands and me with only thousands. Next they'll be making him their king!" So from that time on Saul kept a jealous eye on David. The very next day a tormenting spirit from God overwhelmed Saul, and he began to rave in his house like a madman. David was playing the harp, as he did each day. But Saul had a spear in his hand, and he suddenly hurled it at David, intending to pin him to the wall. But David escaped him twice. (1Sam.18:6-11)

In this text, David, who was anointed but not yet appointed as the next king of Israel, had just defeated the Philistine giant by the name of Goliath. Saul was the current king of Israel, and he'd been rejected by God for partial obedience, which is the same as disobedience in God's eyes. You would think that Saul, the current king, would be trying to mentor David, the future king. However, this was not the case.

After David defeated Goliath, the praise team of Israel started to sing. Their song compared David to Saul. They highlighted that David killed more people than Saul in war. Both Saul and David were fighting for the same team, thus giving Saul a reason to be happy for David. After all, when David did well, all of Israel prospered. Likewise, when Saul did well, all of Israel prospered. Yet, Saul was anything but happy for David. As a matter of fact, Saul was jealous of David and tried to kill him twice. Instead of mentoring David, Saul tried to murder David.

When you are in the fight of your life, you don't need jealous and envious people in your corner. You need people in your corner who want to see you do well. You need people in your corner who take pleasure in your prosperity. You need people in your corner who can remind you that "you can do all things through Christ who strengthens you" (Phil.4:13). You need people in your corner who can remind you that "you are more than a conqueror through Jesus Christ who loves you" (Rom.8:37). You need people in your corner who can remind you, "Greater is he that is in you than he that is in the world" (1Jn.4:4).

This theme of having the right person in your corner plays out well in boxing. Boxers have two key people in their corners. They have a coach who gives them pointers. They also have a cut-man who protects them by bandaging their wounds. When you find yourself in the fight of your life, know that God is both your coach and cut-man. He points you in the right direction through his Word. This is why the Scripture says, "Trust in the Lord with all of your heart and lean not to your own understanding. In all your ways, acknowledge him and he shall direct your paths" (Pro.3:5-6). God also protects you through his Word. His Word teaches us, "God is our refuge and strength, an ever-present help in trouble" (Psm.46:1). Are you trying to win the fight of your life without God? Before we talk about people in your corner, is God in your corner?

I don't want to take for granted that God is in your corner as you are reading this book. I also don't want to take for granted that you know how to get God in your corner if he's not already in your corner. Know this:

1. <u>If God is not in your corner, he wants to be.</u> "Look! I stand at the door and knock. If you hear my voice and open the door, I will come in, and we will share a meal together as friends" (Rev.3:20).

2. <u>If God is going to be in your corner, you must invite him in.</u> God is a gentleman. He will not force himself on anyone. He gives us free-will and we have the choice to choose him or reject him. God gave Adam instructions in the Garden of Eden. Adam and Eve had the choice to obey or reject those instructions (Gen.3).

3. <u>If God is going to come into your corner, you must confess your sins.</u> Confession means to agree with. We must agree that we are sinners in need of the Savior. When we confess our sins, God doesn't hold it against us. He's faithful and just to forgive us and cleanse us of all unrighteousness (1Jn.1:9).

4. <u>If God is going to come into your corner, you must believe in his death, burial, and resurrection, AND invite him to be the Lord of your life.</u> If you confess with your mouth that Jesus is Lord and believe in your heart that God raised Jesus from the dead, you shall be saved (Rom.10:9). Jesus does not just want to be in your life. He wants control of your life. This is what it means to make him Lord. We get out of the driver's seat of our lives and allow Jesus to drive. We surrender our passions, our will, our thoughts, and our actions to Jesus. It's not about what we want. It's about what Jesus wants for us. It's not our actions that save us. It's

about what we believe about Jesus that saves us: our belief in his death, burial, and resurrection.

5. <u>If God is going to control your corner, you must be saved and SURRENDERED.</u> Many people are saved but are not surrendered to the power of the Holy Spirit. Emmanuel is God with us (Mt.1:23). The Holy Spirit is God in us (Acts 2:1-4). The whole world has Emmanuel. Only saved people have the Holy Spirit. The Holy Spirit is not an "it." He's an actual person that Jesus sent in his physical absence to take up residence inside of our bodies to empower us (Acts 1:8), gift us (1Cor.12), change our character (Gal.5:22-23), comfort us and teach us (Jn.14-16), pray for us (Rom.8:26), convict us (Jn.16:8), and to overtake/baptize us (Acts 1:5).

Let's talk a little bit more about who should and who shouldn't be in your corner. Before you can get the right people in your corner, you must get the wrong people out of your corner.

Blessed is the man who walks not in the counsel of the ungodly, nor stands in the way of sinners, nor sits in the seat of the scornful. But his delight is in the law of the Lord, and in his law does he meditate both day and night. And he shall be like a tree planted by the rivers of water, that brings forth his fruit in his season. His leaf shall not wither, and whatever he does shall prosper (Psm.1:1-3).

We are all called to bless people. We are all called to help people. We are all called to lift people. However, when we are in the fight of our lives, we must be selective about who's within our corner. Anyone who ignores God and does not esteem his ways has no business being in our corner. This equates to being ungodly. Anyone who does not know God has no business being in my corner. This equates to a sinner. A sinner is not someone who does wrong. A sinner is someone who doesn't know God. Anyone who mocks God has no business being in my corner. This equates to a scoffer.

At the same time, there is an extreme difference between those who are in my life, and those who are in my corner. God never said that those who ignore him, who don't know him, and who mock him can't be in our lives. He's telling us that these people can't be in our corner. If those who are far from God are not in our lives, we can't reach them for salvation. You can't reach those with whom you have no relationship. You must ask God for wisdom to know the difference between those who are in your life, and those whom you should grant access to your corner.

If certain people shouldn't have access to my corner, who should? The people who should have access to my corner are those who take pleasure in the Word — not the world. The psalmist is literally telling us that our company matters. Our blessings and happiness are directly contingent upon the company that we keep. Show me your company, and I'll show you your future.

When we are in the fight of our lives, we need people in our corner who encourage us to meditate on God's Word. Meditation is the opposite of worry. When I worry, I think about my problems all day long. When I meditate, I think about God and his Word all day long. Thinking about my problems brings anxiety. Thinking about God's Word brings peace. Are you anxious? Is the enemy stealing your peace by causing you to think about the "what ifs" of life? If so, switch your focus from worry to the Word and experience the joy of God's peace overtaking you. "You will keep in perfect peace all who trust you, all whose thoughts are fixed on you" (Isa.26:3)! Peace is not the absence of a fight. Peace is the presence of God in the midst of the fight. I don't have to wait until my fight is over to have peace. I already have peace right now because God is with me.

There are four benefits to having the right person(s), who direct you to God's Word, in your corner:

1. <u>The Word PLANTS me.</u> "He'll be like a tree planted by the rivers of water" (Psm.1:3). Satan wants to use your fight to uproot you. He wants to uproot you from your family, church family, friends, destiny, dreams, God's promises, and so much more. Satan has already had a

sneak preview into your future and doesn't want you to experience all of the wonderful things that God has in store for you. However, when you are in the Word, you remain planted—even in the middle of a severe fight. You may bend, but you will not break. You "remain steadfast, unmovable, always abounding in the work of the Lord; know that your labor is not in vain in the Lord" (1Cor.15:58).

2. The Word makes me PRODUCTIVE. "He'll bring forth his fruit in his season" (Psm.1:3). Your productivity is connected to you being planted. When you are planted in the Word and a local assembly of believers, you produce fruit. It's not enough to be planted in the Word. You must also be planted in a local church. You can't love God but hate his wife, the church. Christian productivity is two-fold; it is seen in my character (love, joy, peace, patience, goodness, faithfulness, gentleness, kindness, and self-control (Gal.5:22-23) and in me producing other Christians (Jn.15:1-8).

3. The Word makes me PERSEVERE. "His leaf shall not wither" (Psm.1:3). Leaves blossom and wither according to natural seasons. In the fall and winter, leaves wither away and die. In the spring and summer, leaves blossom and turn pretty colors. It's important to

stay in the Word, especially when you are in the fight of your life. When we do, we find the strength to keep striving for God's promises over our lives no matter what season we are in. We find strength to continue obeying God no matter what season we are in.

4. <u>The Word makes me PROSPER.</u> "And whatever he does shall prosper" (Psm.1:3). Prosperity is not a cuss word. It's a misunderstood word. I don't know anyone who doesn't want to prosper at the core of his or her heart. I don't know anyone who wants to fail. Prosperity does not mean that we don't have problems. Prosperity doesn't mean that we don't have fights. It means that God gives us the strength to go through or go over our fights. You really don't know how prosperous you are until you are in the fight of your life. When you are in the fight of your life and you have the God-given strength to get through it no matter how tough things are, you are prosperous! When you are in the fight of your life and you have the God-given fortitude to go over your fight no matter how hard it is, you are prosperous!

I'm so grateful that God has placed the right people in my corner to help me win the fights of my life. When I was distant from my father (whom I'm now really close to) and

I didn't know what to think of my step-father, God sent my grandfather, Dr. Tommy Chappell, to teach me about life, manhood, and most importantly my relationship with Christ. When my marriage was on the brink of divorce and my family was falling apart, God sent a human angel to minister to us and carry us through that season. When New Rising Star Church was at a crossroads, God sent an entire congregation of people to help carry us through the transition. When fighting the betrayal of those who used to be friends and internal battles of getting better and not bitter, God sent so many people of whom I can't name them all without missing somebody.

The bottom line is this: there is no way possible to win the fight of your life without the right person in your corner. God must be in your corner, and those who are in the Word must be in your corner. Remember that boxers go to the corner between rounds. When the boxer is between rounds, conflict ceases, but the fight is not over. Thank God for periods of peace when the attacks of Satan are non-existent or not as intense. At the same time, never mistake your fight for being over when you are just between rounds. "Submit yourself to God, resist the devil, and he will flee" (Jms.4:7). Satan flees for a season, but he does return. When Satan leaves and things are calm, go to your spiritual corner/ prayer. Talk to God through prayer, and allow God to talk back to you through his Word. When Satan returns and things get chaotic, don't be afraid to get into the ring and heed/ practice God's Word. With the right Word from the right corner, we win the fight of our lives!

It's Time to Throw Hands

- Do I have the right people on earth in my corner to win this fight?
- Is God in my corner?
- Have I given God free reign in my corner, or am I using him as a mere figurehead?
- Am I open to guidance, or do I think and act as if I know everything?

-Prayer:

Lord Jesus, remove the wrong people from my corner. Place the right people in my corner. Open my heart to receive your guidance directly from you and your Word, or indirectly from those you send my way, in Jesus' name, AMEN!

CHAPTER 6

This Fight Is Not My Fault?

There is an extreme difference between persecution and chastisement. On the surface, they look the same because both of them involve challenge, struggle, trouble, hardship, fighting, and much more. At the same time, they are totally different. Persecution is when I find myself in the fight of my life for doing something right. Perhaps I stood for my faith in Jesus Christ, and it brought about hardship in my life. Chastisement is when I find myself in the fight of my life for doing something wrong. Maybe God warned me of something, and I didn't take heed to the warning; therefore, I find myself having to deal with consequences that could have been avoided.

When I find myself in the fight of my life because of

persecution, whatever I did to get in it is what I must keep doing to get out of it. When I find myself in the fight of my life because of chastisement, whatever I did to get in it is what I must reassess, reexamine, and repent in order to get out of it. In other words, sometimes, obeying God will cause you to be in the fight of your life. Obedience to God may cause you to make unpopular decisions that afflict the comfortable and comfort the afflicted. When this is the case, I must remember that if obedience got me in it, then obedience will get me out of it. Sometimes, disobedience to God will cause me to get into the fight of my life. If disobedience got me in it, then obedience will get me out of it.

The Bible is filled with examples of those who found themselves in the fight of their lives because of persecution. They were children of God who stood for God. Their stance afflicted the comfortable and comforted the afflicted. They found themselves in the hardships of life because of their stance. Here are a few examples:

1. The 3 Hebrew Boys In The Fiery Furnace (Dan.3):

In the time of Babylonian captivity, King Nebuchadnezzar built an image of gold over ninety feet tall. He commanded everyone in the land to bow down to the image at the sound of the music. In essence, the king commanded everyone to worship the idol. This same scenario is playing out in today's culture. Cultural artists are building ungodly images inside of their music; whether they be images of sex outside of marriage, drugs, violence, get-rich-quick illegal schemes, immoral lifestyles etc. At the sound of the music via radio, MTV, VH-1, BET, and more, many people are bowing to these images.

Although everyone in the land bowed, three Hebrew boys named Shadrach, Meshach, and Abednego refused to bow. To bow to this image of gold would be to be disloyal to Yahweh, the one and only true God. When they refused to bow, King Nebuchadnezzar had them thrown into a fiery furnace. They found themselves in the fight of their lives in the middle of the fire, not for doing wrong, but for doing something right. They found themselves in the fight of their lives because of persecution. They stood for God, and it got them in trouble.

King Nebuchadnezzar went to check on them and noticed something. He put three in the fire, but he saw four walking around loose, and the fourth one looked like the Son of God. Obedience to God didn't keep them from fire, but it caused Jesus to get inside of the fire with them. Make no mistake about it. Obedience to God does not keep us from the fight of our lives. It causes God to be with us in the fight of our lives.

When Shadrach, Meshach, and Abednego came out of the fire, their hair was not singed, their clothes were not burned, and they didn't smell like smoke. Because God was with them in the fire, he protected them. Therefore, when they came out of the fire, they didn't look like what they had been through.

When God is with you in the fight of your life, he protects you. Therefore, you don't look like what you've been through when you come out of the fight of your life.

When the three Hebrew boys came out of the fire, King Nebuchadnezzar acknowledged that no other god could save like the god of Shadrach, Meshach, and Abednego. God used their fight to make himself known to others. This is exactly what God wants to do in your life. Your fight is not even for you. It's so others can see God in you and through you. When they see God fight for you and move in your life, it will cause them to believe on the God that you serve.

2. Daniel In The Lion's Den (Dan. 6):

The prophet named Daniel, who worked for the Babylonian government, had a spirit of excellence. Because of his excellent spirit, the king made plans to place him over the entire empire. His co-workers were not happy about his promotion, so they schemed to bring him down. Because they couldn't find anything against him concerning his work ethic, they conspired to bring him down because of his religion. The king signed a 30-day decree that anyone who prayed to anyone divine or human other than the king would be thrown into a den of lions.

When Daniel heard about the decree signed by the king, he went home and prayed while kneeling down towards Jerusalem with the window open the same way that he had always done. Because of this, Daniel found himself in the fight of his life, thrown into the middle of a den of lions. He was in trouble, not for doing something wrong, but for doing something right. Persecution caused the fight of Daniel's life.

When the king went to check on Daniel, he learned that Daniel was still alive. God sent an angel to shut the mouths of the lions. Obedience to God didn't keep Daniel from the lion's den. It protected Daniel while he was in the lion's den. Obedience to God doesn't keep you from the fight of your life; however, it will cause God to be with you and protect you while in the fight of your life. As a result, the king acknowledged that the God of Daniel was the only true and living God. Again, God uses the fight of our lives to make himself known to the entire world. When others see how God moves in your fight, it causes them to want to know him, love him, and serve him as well.

3. Job's Suffering (Job):

Job had everything that anybody could ever dream of having on earth. He had character. Job was a good and upright man who respected God and avoided evil (Job 1:1). He had children. Job had seven sons and three daughters (Job 1:2). He had capital. He had much substance and was considered to be the greatest of all in the East (Job 1:3). Last, he had crisis. In one day, Job lost everything including his substance and his children (Job 1:13-19).

After losing everything, Job found himself in the fight of his life; and he'd done nothing wrong. No matter how much character you have, it doesn't stop your crisis. No matter how many children you have to take care of you, it doesn't stop your crisis. No matter how much capital you have, it doesn't stop your crisis. It's possible to live right and still find yourself in the fight of your life.

Job responded by worshiping God. How do you worship God when you've lost everything? You would think that Job passed his test when he received double for his trouble (Job 42). However he passed his test, long before being restored, when he worshiped God after losing everything (Job 1:20). Satan told God that Job only worshiped him because of how God blessed Job (Job 1). Satan also told God that Job would curse him to his face if God took everything away from Job (Job 1). The fact that Job responded by worshiping God instead cursing God shows us that Job was mature in his faith and didn't flunk the test. Anybody can worship God when things are well, but can you worship God in the middle of your fight?

Job had to get the wrong people out of his corner and the right people in his corner to win the fight. His wife told him to curse God and die (Job 2:9). His friends made improper assumptions about his life and told him that he was in this fight because he'd done something wrong (Job 4-37). God answered all of Job's questions with questions, rebuking

Job during his suffering (Job 38-41). Job had to block out the counsel of his wife and friends to heed the counsel of God.

As a result of hearing God's counsel, Job prayed for the same friends who made improper assumptions about his life (Job 42:10). The Lord also restored Job double what he lost (Job 42:12), and Job lived 140 years after God restored him double (Job 42:16). Not only can God restore what Satan stole from you in your fight, God can also give you time to enjoy his restoration. The point of the matter is that, like Job, we can live for God and still find ourselves in the fight of our lives. When we've done nothing to cause our fight, consider it persecution. If serving God got us in it, serving God will get us out of it.

4. <u>David In The Valley (Psm.23):</u>

The 23rd Psalm is one of the most popular passages of Scripture in all the world. King David found himself in the fight of his life in the middle of a dark valley, not for doing something wrong, but for doing something right. David said, "He leads me in the paths of righteousness for his namesake." Immediately after this statement, David said, "Though I walk through the valley of the shadow of death, I will fear no evil. For God is with me. His rod and staff comfort me." Why did David talk about a dark valley, just after he talked about a righteous path? Here's the lesson: sometimes a righteous path can lead you through a dark valley. Sometimes doing the right thing can cause you to find yourself in the fight of your life.

Obedience to God didn't keep David from the valley. It didn't keep David from the fight of his life. Obedience to God caused God to be with David while in the fight of his life. God does not keep his children from the fights of their lives. However, he is always with his children in the fights of their lives.

5. Paul In The Prison (Phil. 4):

Paul was formally known as Saul. As Saul, he persecuted the church. As Saul, he held the coats of the people who stoned Stephen, one of the first deacons inside of the church. He met Jesus on the Damascus road, and it changed his life. There is no way possible to have a real encounter with Jesus Christ and not change your life. One encounter with Jesus will change your entire mind, heart, soul, spirit, and actions. Many people attend church but have still not encountered Christ. This is why we leave the same way every Sunday. We walk the same, talk the same, think the same, live the same, and act the same. God is not interested in people checking a religious box that stacks up to a "to do" list. He wants to radically turn our lives right-side up. Our lives were already upside down. This can only be done when we encounter him.

When Saul threatened the church and persecuted the church, he never went to prison. When he met Jesus and his name was changed to Paul, it seems like he stayed in the prison. He often went to prison for preaching the gospel of Jesus Christ. Doing the right thing by standing for Jesus ultimately caused him to be thrown into prison in the fight his life on several occasions.

Such was the case when Paul wrote to the church at Philippi. He wrote this letter from prison. He was in prison for preaching the gospel. He found himself in the fight of his life for doing right, which equates to persecution. While in prison, he encouraged the church at Philippi to rejoice, be kind, not to worry, pray, be thankful, and much more. Take a moment and put yourself in Paul's shoes. First, nobody wants to go to prison. If you went to prison, you would at least want to know that you went for doing something wrong. If you went to prison for doing right, perhaps you would have an attitude of bitterness. If you were in this predicament, wouldn't you need encouragement?

When Paul needed encouragement, he encouraged other people. How did he have the strength to do this? He did this because God was with him. Paul was in the fight of his life, and he needed encouragement; yet, he had power to encourage others. Once again, obedience to God doesn't keep us from the fight of our lives; it causes God to be with us in the fight of our lives. When God is with you, you can do the impossible. When God is with you, you can do the unthinkable!

6. Jesus On The Cross (The Gospels):

Jesus did good to others and for others his entire life on earth. He healed the sick, raised the dead, gave sight to the blind, unstopped deaf ears, and much more. He was absolutely amazing. He showed himself to be Lord over nature; a meteorologist who predicted weather and caused the elements to obey him (Mk.4:35-41). He showed himself to be Lord over demons; a psychiatrist who casted out a legion of demons from a man, causing him to return to his right mind (Mk.5:1-19). He showed himself to be Lord over sickness; a gynecologist who healed a woman that had been bleeding on her menstrual cycle for twelve long years (Mk.5:20-34). He showed himself to be Lord over death; a pediatrician who raised the daughter of Jairus from the dead (Mk.5:35-43).

In spite of all of the good that Jesus did, at the end of his life he found himself on an old rugged cross dying a death that he did not deserve to pay a debt that we could not pay. Even Jesus was in the fight of his life; not for doing wrong, but for doing right. How could people not like him, and he did nothing but good? His good often afflicted the comfortable and comforted the afflicted. Yet as he hung on the cross, his father was with him. He spoke to his Father while hanging on the cross. He asked his Father to forgive his perpetrators (Lk. 23:34). He told his Father that the work he'd been given to pay for the sins of humanity was now finished (Jn.19:30). He told his Father that he was putting his Spirit into the hands of his

Father (Lk. 23:46).

Obedience to the Father didn't keep Jesus from the fight of his life on the cross. It caused the Father to be with him while in of the fight of his life. Now let me address the elephant in the room. If the Father was with Jesus the entire time, why did Jesus say, "My God, My God, why have you abandoned me?" (Mt. 27:46). Jesus was not using random words. He was actually quoting Scripture. David, perhaps while in a cave, was the first to say this (Psm. 22:1). Jesus, the Son of David, said it on the cross. Here's the point. When you find yourself in the fight of your life, you need Scripture to make it through. Here's the second point. For God to "Forgive them" (Jesus' first prayer), he had to forsake him. If the people were not going to pay for their own sins, somebody had to pay. The Father completely satisfied his wrath for the world by taking it out on his own Son, Jesus the Christ. When it feels like God has left you in the fight of your life, know that he always has a greater purpose.

Here's a quick recap. When you are in the fight of your life and you did nothing to cause it, consider it persecution. In this case, ask God to convict by you the power of his Holy Spirit in the area of righteousness, that you may continue to do right even when it causes hardship. When persecution is the cause of your fight, whatever you did to get in it is what you must keep doing to get out of it.

It's Time to Throw Hands

- Did I do anything that God is pleased with to cause this fight?
- If pleasing God got me into this fight, has it changed my view of God?
- Am I bitter towards God?
- If so, have I been honest with God about the feelings he already knows are in my heart?

-Prayer:

Lord, give me a heart that desires to please you at all times in all circumstances. When pleasing you brings about a fight, give me the conviction and the strength to stand strong, in Jesus' name, AMEN!

CHAPTER 7
I Brought This Fight On Myself!

In the previous chapter, I provided six examples of people who found themselves in the fight of their lives because of persecution. However, sometimes we are in the fight of our lives and it's not persecution. Sometimes, we cause it on ourselves. What happens when I can't blame my situation or circumstance on Satan, friends, family, haters, or anyone else? What happens when I'm in the fight of my life because of my own bad decisions and my own poor choices? Such is the case with Israel, God's chosen people, in Judges 6.

[1]The Israelites did evil in the Lord's sight. So the Lord handed them over to the Midianites for seven years . . . .[7-10]When they cried out to the Lord because of Midian, the Lord sent a prophet to the

Israelites. He said, "This is what the Lord, the God of Israel, says: I brought you up out of slavery in Egypt. I rescued you from the Egyptians and from all who oppressed you. I drove out your enemies and gave you their land. I told you, 'I am the Lord your God. You must not worship the gods of the Amorites, in whose land you now live.' But you have not listened to me."

The entire nation of Israel found themselves in the fight of their lives. This fight was not caused by persecution. Rather, this fight was God's chastisement of his children because of their disobedience to God in the area of idol worship. In response to their continued disobedience, the Lord gave them into the hands of their enemies.

Not only did God deliver Israel into the hand of the Midians, he allowed them to stay there for a set period of seven years. Seven is a metaphor for completion. After completing the earth, God rested on the seventh day (Gen.2:2). In the Old Testament, animals had to be seven days old before being used for sacrifice (Ex.22:30). Naaman, the leper, had to dip in the Jordan River seven times for his healing to be complete (2Kg.5:10). Joshua led Israel to march around Jericho seven days before the walls fell down (Jo.6:3-4). After being married and divorced five times and shacking with the sixth man; the woman at the well met the seventh man named Jesus, and her entire life was changed (Jn.4).

The fact that God left Israel in the hands of Midian for seven years tells us that he didn't deliver them until their suffering was complete. When you find yourself in the fight of your life, God won't deliver you until your suffering is complete. Often, we kick, scream, and holler, but God doesn't take us out until we are done. Have you ever be hungry and heated a microwave meal to curb your hunger? The directions said three minutes, but you took it out too early. As a result, you ate uncooked food and ended up getting sick. Likewise, when God delivers us prematurely, we are undone and make other people sick. We fail to learn the lesson and don't realize the severity of our actions. We fail the test and flunk the lesson, thus having to repeat the class over and over and over. For many of us, this year's fight is not a new fight. It's a repeat fight that we caused on ourselves because we exited prematurely the last time.

Instead of us focusing on what is happening to us, we must focus on what God is doing inside of us. God uses our trials and hardships to develop patience in us. It is not what happens to us that brings us joy. Rather, it's what God is doing inside of us that brings us joy. This is why James, Jesus' half brother, teaches us:

Dear brothers and sisters, when troubles of any kind come your way, consider it an opportunity for great joy. For you know that when your faith is tested, your endurance/patience has a chance to grow. So let it grow, for when your endurance/patience is fully developed, you will be perfect and complete, needing nothing (Jm. 1:2-4).

The fight of our lives doesn't feel good; however, God is working it out for our good. God works even our worse fights for our good by using them to shape us into his image (see Rom. 8:28-29).

I'm a living witness that you can sometimes cause the fight of your life on yourself. I'm also a living witness that God will shape you into his image in the middle of your pain. At twenty-eight years old, I became the pastor of New Rising Star Church in Birmingham, Alabama on May 2010. I succeeded my grandfather, Dr. Tommy C. Chappell, after he served thirty-five years as the pastor from 1975 to 2010. The only time I left New Rising Star Church was to go to college at Kentucky State University from 2000to 2004, where I attended Mt. Calvary Baptist Church under the leadership of Dr. Felix G. Williams III. I was considered the golden child. My mother is a judge and my grandfather was the pastor of a thriving ministry. Mom kept people out of jail. Grandfather kept people out of hell. When I went to college, I met the love of my life who already had three children. I married her and brought her back home to Birmingham, Alabama. I brought her back home to a traditional church. Our traditions were not wrong; my wife and I just grew up two different ways. We both had expectations according to how we grew up. Many times, I elevated things that were just differences to levels of being right and wrong. This is how one of the major fights of my life started.

Many people at my home church had an idea of who I should and should not marry. Even if they didn't know who I should marry, they didn't think that I should have married a woman who already had kids. He's the golden child. Why did he marry her? He has a future (as if she didn't). Why did he marry her? On top of marrying a woman who already had children, it was also a fight serving in a traditional setting. My grandmother, the pastor's wife, dressed a certain way. She sat on the first or second row during service, wore hats, and much more. The majority of pastors' wives did this in the south. This wasn't a bad tradition. It showed support, unspoken leadership, and many other things.

I was being groomed to be the pastor, but my wife didn't fit the mold of what everyone thought she should be. She liked being behind the scenes, but everyone wanted her to be visible and to conform to what they were used to seeing. Women wore white on the first Sunday. She didn't understand why we had this tradition so she didn't do it. I have always believed that people should serve in God's house according to how God gifts them. However, I didn't examine until later that being a minister's wife or deacon's wife was the only way that women served; because their husbands were in office, not because God gifted them for certain required duties.

I was not mature enough to cover my wife. Rather than allow her the freedom to be herself and to grow at her own pace, I attempted to force her to conform. This drove a deep wedge in our marriage and relationship. I didn't want the pressure on me, so I transferred the unspoken pressure that I was feeling to her. I remember being so angry at her for not conforming. I let the sun go down on my wrath and allowed Satan an open door into my life (Eph. 4:26-27). One day, my wife called me over twenty times to attempt to gain understanding, work things out, and move forward. I wouldn't even pick up the phone. I sent her short text messages back and said very unkind and unchristian words. The next day I came home from work, and she was gone—she and our children.

We were separated, and I played a major part in the cause of it by staying angry. For the first few weeks, I lived a lie. Everyone asked, "Where is your wife?" I replied, "She's sick, so she didn't come." I jokingly say today that I used up all my sick days. After I said that she was sick one too many times, I couldn't use that excuse anymore. One of the best things that could have ever happened was for the cat to get out of the bag and people know that we were separated. I felt liberated that I no longer had to live a lie and that I could actually go get help.

The devil was whispering in my ear the entire time. "Get a divorce. Find a new wife. Start over." Jesus reminded me that "whoever saves his life shall lose it, and whoever loses his life for my sake shall find it" (Mt. 16:25). Logic said that divorce would save your life and free you from shame. Faith said, lose your life in obedience to God, and you'll find it later. Jesus also reminded me that you can't rule God's house if you can't rule your own house (1Tim. 3:5). It was during this time of separation that God truly started to work on me. I stopped trying to make my wife the right person and started trying to be the right person. I didn't realize how broken and warped I really was. I was religious, ritualistic, and my traditions made the word of God of no effect (Mk. 7:13); not because they were bad traditions, but because I elevated them as being gospel truth.

No matter how much I wanted to be delivered from this fight, God had a set time. He wouldn't take us out until we were done. He wouldn't put us back together until we were complete. I remember vividly lying on the floor prostrate during this time and crying out to God. God literally spoke to me in an audible voice. It wasn't deep. He said "1 Peter 5:10." I looked this Scripture up and it said, ". . . after you've suffered a while, God will make you perfect, establish, strengthen, and settle you." God completes us, strengthens us, establishes us, and settles us in our suffering. This is just what God did. People saw my wife and I publicly separated. They also had a front row seat to watch God resurrect our marriage on Resurrection Sunday/Easter.

When you are in the fight of your life, don't focus on what is happening to you. Focus on what God is doing inside of you. Not only is God developing patience, but he is also shaping us into his image. This is why Paul said:

And we know that all things work together for good to them that love God, to them who are the called according to his purpose. For whom he did foreknow, he also did predestinate to be conformed to the image of his Son, that he might be the firstborn among many brethren (Rom. 8:28-29).

How can the fight of my life work for my good when it's painful, lonely, time-consuming, and much more? How can this terrible fight work for my good when my children have gone astray, sickness seems incurable, marriage is on the rocks, and poverty seems to take over amongst many other things? God takes what doesn't feel good and works it for our good. Before he changes our fight, he uses our fight to change us. God uses our fight to shape us into his image. When the fight is over, we look like Jesus, walk like Jesus, talk like Jesus, and have more and more of his character.

What doesn't feel good works for our good by causing us to look more like Jesus Christ. If you are honest, your fights taught you how to pray. Your fights taught you how to worship. Your fights taught you how to draw close to God. Your fights taught you how to fast. Your fights taught you how to praise. Instead of feeling sorry about your fight, go ahead and tell God, "Thank You!" Were it not for the fight, you wouldn't and couldn't be whom God has made you to be.

It's Time to Throw Hands

- Did I do anything that God is not pleased with to cause this fight?
- If so, what did I do?
- What corrections do I need to make within myself to win this fight?
- Have I surrendered my errors to God for him to correct, or am I trying to change myself?
- Do I believe that God can and will help me, even if I caused this on myself?

-Prayer:

Lord I thank you so much for your mercy that holds back what I really deserve. Thank you for another chance. I surrender all of shortcomings to you. Correct me from the inside out, and fill me with your patience not to rush your process of correction in Jesus' name, AMEN!

CHAPTER 8

God Wants to Help You

There are some fights that you can't get out of on your own. The problem is not that we need help. It's admitting that we need help. This requires humility. Whenever you are in the fight of your life, remember that God resists the proud but gives grace to the humble (1 Pet. 5:5).

In Judges 6, Israel was the cause of their own fight. They continued to disobey God in the area of idol worship, and God turned them over into the hand of the Midianite people. Although Israel was the cause of their own fight, God raised up Gideon to deliver his children.

And Israel was greatly impoverished because of the Midianites; and the children of Israel cried unto the Lord . . . And there came an angel of the Lord, and sat under an oak which was in Ophrah, that pertained unto Joash the Abiezrite: and his son Gideon threshed wheat by the winepress, to hide it from the Midianites. And the angel of the Lord appeared unto him, and said unto him, The Lord is with thee, thou mighty man of valour. And Gideon said unto him, Oh my Lord, if the Lord be with us, why then is all this befallen us? And where be all his miracles which our fathers told us of, saying, Did not the Lord bring us up from Egypt? But now the Lord has forsaken us, and delivered us into the hands of the Midianites. And the Lord looked upon him, and said, Go in this thy might, and thou shalt save Israel from the hand of the Midianites: have not I sent you? And he said unto him, Oh my Lord, wherewith shall I save Israel? Behold, my family is poor in Manasseh and I am the least in my father's house. And the Lord said unto him, Surely I will be with you, and you shall smite the Midianites as one man (Jdg. 6:6,11-16).

This passage teaches us several things.

(1.) <u>The Call Of Those Who Help Is Always Connected To The Cry Of Those In Hurt.</u> Israel was suffering in a major way. Their suffering made them cry out to God. When they cried out to God because of hurt, God called Gideon to help. The call of God's leader is always connected to the cry of his people.

If God calls you to an assignment, it is never about you.

God does not call us because we are so gifted. God doesn't call us because we are so wonderful. God doesn't call us because we have it all together. God calls us to help those who are hurting. If people don't hurt, they won't cry out to God. If they don't cry out to God, God won't call us. This doesn't mean that God doesn't give us attributes to serve. It just means that God gifts us in a justifiable order. God doesn't call us because we are qualified; he qualifies us because he calls us. God doesn't call us because we are gifted. God gifts us because he calls us. It's never about us. It's all about God and helping his hurting people.

(2.) <u>Our Merciful God Wants To Help Us, Even When We Cause Our Own Fight.</u> Not only does God want to help us; he wants to help us even when we're the cause of our own fight. Israel caused their own fight, yet God raised up Gideon to deliver them. This speaks to the mercy of God. God's goodness gives us what we do not deserve. God's mercy holds back what we really do deserve. God could have taken the attitude, "My children caused this on themselves, so I'll let them lay in the bed they made forever." Although God didn't want to see his children suffer, he allowed them to suffer to turn their hearts back to him. When their hearts were completely turned to him, God delivered.

If you have ever been the cause of your own fight, don't allow Satan to condemn you any longer. You are still God's child. God has not thrown you away. People may throw you away, but God will put you in a recycling bin to use you over and over and over. I know that you think you don't deserve help. None of us do. We have all deliberately disobeyed God. Thank God that his anger endures but a moment (Psm. 30:5). Instead of being mad at you, God got mad at his son, Jesus. Instead of satisfying his wrath upon you, God satisfied his wrath with his son Jesus. God is not mad when he corrects us. He simply corrects us to yield the peaceable fruit of righteousness in our lives because he loves us more than we could ever imagine.

- (3.) <u>When God Sends Help, It May Not Look The Way We Think It Should Look.</u> Out of all of the people that God could call to deliver Israel, God called Gideon. Gideon was not qualified to deliver Israel because:

    a) <u>Gideon was working himself out of a hole.</u>
    Gideon was threshing wheat in a winepress when God called him. Farmers normally thresh wheat in open places on a hill. After grinding/sifting the wheat, they throw it in the air, allowing the wind to separate the wheat (useable part) from the chaff (unusable part). Instead of sifting wheat on a hill in

an open place, Gideon sifted wheat in a wine press. A wine press is a dark hole. Gideon was working, yet he was working from a hole when he normally would have been on a hill.

God really has a sense of humor. Why would he call someone to help me in the fight of my life when the one he calls is working himself or herself out of their own hole? This doesn't make sense. God uses the foolish things of the world to confound the wise and the weak things of the world to confound the strong (1Cor. 1:27). God uses people who are most likely to succeed so that he can get all the glory. Stay open minded. Treat everyone right. You never know whom God is going to use to help you win the fight of your life.

b) <u>Gideon came from a poor family.</u>
Even Gideon was shocked that God would use him to deliver Israel. Immediately, Gideon started to point out his deficiencies, one of them being that he was poor. Though Gideon pointed out his deficiencies, God called him a mighty man of valor. When God calls us to an assignment, we must learn to see ourselves the way that God sees us.

God uses even poor people. He used a widow to take care of his prophet Elijah (1Kg. 17). This lady lost her income because she lost her husband. On top of this, the land was in a famine. Yet God used her in spite of poverty. There is no excuse for not answering the phone when God calls you. When will you stop sending him to voicemail?

c) <u>Gideon was the youngest in his family.</u>
Gideon responded to God's call by saying, "I'm the least in my family." Least means the youngest. Somehow, Gideon thought that being young would disqualify him from God using him. With God, age is nothing but a number. Aaliyah, the great musical genius, wrote a song that echoed the same words.

God uses people of all ages. God used young people in biblical history. At seventeen, Joseph had a dream (Gen. 37). As a youth, David fought Goliath (1Sam. 17). Solomon built the temple at a young age (1Kg. 3). At eight years old, Josiah became king of Judah (2Kg. 22). As a teenager, Mary birthed Jesus (Mt. 2). As a youth, Timothy led the church in Ephesus (1Tim. 4:12). God also used old people. Caleb was as strong at eighty-five as he was when Moses sent him out (Jos. 14:11). Old men dreamed dreams (Joel 2, Acts 2). Anna was eighty-four when she confirmed Jesus as the Messiah (Lk. 2:38).

The point of it all is this: when you are in the fight of your life, it may surprise you to see who God uses to help you. God can use whomever, whenever, and however he chooses. God doesn't need anyone's permission to use people for his good and his glory. God doesn't report to a board or an authority. He's God all by himself. Ask God, "Lord, please keep my eyes and my heart open." The worst thing you can do is reject God-sent help because it didn't come in the package you were expecting.

It's Time to Throw Hands

- Have I humbled myself to admit that I need help?
- In what ways has God sent help in expected ways?
- In what ways has God sent help in unexpected ways?
- Have I rejected or received God's help?

-Prayer:

Lord, thank you for being willing to help me in all of my fights, even when I cause it on myself. Help me to humble myself and admit I need your help. Help me to be open to receiving your help. Help me to recognize your help in expected and unexpected ways, in Jesus' name, AMEN!

CHAPTER 9

From Pain to Paradise

To say that the fight of your life is painful is an understatement. If it weren't painful, it wouldn't be the fight of your life. It would just be a fight. At the end of Jesus' public ministry, he found himself in the fight of his life on an old, rugged cross. Despite his many miracles, his miracles were not his purpose. His purpose was to die to save his people from their sins (Mt. 1:21). On the surface at first glance, it seems as if Jesus was in the fight of his life for no reason at all. At second glance, we learn that the fight of Jesus' life was connected to his purpose. If his purpose was to die to save his people from their sins (Mt. 1:21), and he died on the cross in the fight of his life, it's safe to say that the fight of Jesus' life was connected to his purpose.

Likewise, sometimes the fight of our lives is connected to our God-ordained purpose. When this is the case, the fight of our lives cannot be avoided. No matter how much we try to get around it, it's inevitable that we have to go through it. Jesus prayed the same prayer three times in the Garden of Gethsemane. "Father, if it be possible, let this cup pass from me. Nevertheless, not my will, but thy will be done" (Mt. 26:36-46). Jesus was saying to his Father, 'If there is any other way to save people, reveal it to me. I want to save people, but I don't want to die on the cross.' The Father never released Jesus, his Son, from the pain of the cross. Ultimately, the silence of the Father was a "No." Jesus surrendered his will to his Father and went to the cross. When God says "No," it's because what we ask him will stop us from fulfilling our God-given purpose.

I believe that everyone is born with the same purpose. We just fulfill it in different ways according to how God gifts us individually. Our purpose is to bring God glory by knowing him and making him known to the entire world. God receives glory when we make him known to the entire world. We can't make him known if we don't know him ourselves. Therefore, walking in purpose begins with both my natural and supernatural gifts. At my first birth, I get natural gifts. At my second birth when I accept Jesus Christ as my personal Lord and Savior, I get supernatural gifts (1Cor. 12). Once I discover my gifts, I know my passion. My passion leads to my profession. The goal is to make a living doing something that I absolutely love to do. My profession leads to my platform. When I'm good at what I do, it gives me a circle of influence. People listen to me and seek my advice just because I'm revered in my profession. My platform leads to my purpose. Once I have a circle of influence, it's my responsibility to point all glory back to God by making Jesus known to the world. It's the equivalent of letting my light shine before men so they can see my good works and glorify my Father in Heaven (Mt. 5:16). Jesus fulfilled his God-given purpose in connection to the pain of the cross. His purpose caused pain, but at the end of the pain was paradise.

Jesus was on the cross because the fight of his life was connected to his purpose (Lk. 23:39-43). The thieves who hung beside Jesus were on the cross because the fight of their lives was connected to them being the problem. Jesus did nothing wrong to be hung on the cross. He was guilty of walking in purpose. The thieves were being punished because of what they had stolen. Jesus was in the fight of his life on the cross because he was convicted by his purpose. The thieves were in the fight of their lives on the cross because they were being corrected for their problems. Sometimes, the fight of my life is because of my God-given convictions. Other times, the fight of my life is because of God's correction. Regardless of why I'm in the fight of my life, it is painful.

It's helpful to remember these three things while in the fight of your life:

1. <u>I don't have to prove myself.</u>

Many people, including one of the thieves who hung beside Jesus on the cross, questioned his identity. The thieves mocked Jesus and said, "If you are the Christ, save yourself and us" (Lk. 23:39-43). Jesus didn't succumb to the request of people to prove himself. This wasn't the first time that Jesus' identity was questioned. His identity was first questioned at the beginning of his public ministry. After Jesus' baptism, the Spirit led Jesus up into the wilderness to be tempted of the devil (Mt. 4). Every temptation began with this challenge: "If you are the Son of God," do this or do that. Satan wanted Jesus to question what his Father had said about him at his baptism. His Father already told him, "This is my beloved Son, in whom I am well pleased" (Mt. 3:16-17).

Logically, I can understand why Satan attacked Jesus' identity. The Father declared that he was pleased with his Son Jesus, but Jesus had yet to do anything yet. The Father declared Jesus as his Son in whom he was well pleased before Jesus ever performed a miracle, gained a mass following, or even began his public ministry. It's easy to question one's identity when they haven't done anything to prove it yet.

I can't understand why the thieves and soldiers attacked Jesus' identity at the end of his public ministry when Jesus was on the cross in the fight of his life. The thief asked Jesus to prove himself (Lk. 23:39-43); this was after Jesus turned water into wine (Jn. 2), after Jesus made the winds and seas obey him (Mk. 4:35-41), after Jesus cast a legion of demons out of a man (Mk. 5:1-20), after Jesus healed a woman who had been bleeding on her menstrual cycle for twelve years (Mk. 5:20-34), after Jesus raised the daughter of Jairus from the dead (Mk. 5:34-43), after Jesus fed five thousand men no counting the women and children (Jn. 6), and after Jesus did many other miracles. No wonder Jesus didn't respond to the thief and others asking him to prove himself. If people didn't believe in who he was as the Christ and the Son of the living God after all of his miracles, there was nothing that Jesus could have done at that moment to make them believe.

Oftentimes, when we are in the fight of our lives, we do things in attempt to prove ourselves to other people. If your track record is good and people still find fault, there is nothing that you can do to prove who you are to them. It's imperative that we hold onto our peace and let God fight our battles. When our godly actions don't show people who we are, God's Spirit will show people who we are in God's time. Stop trying to prove yourself to people who already have their minds made up about you. You are wasting valuable time and energy that you need to get to the place where God wants you to go. You are already who God says you are. Other people just don't know it yet. In time, God will reveal/uncover what is already there about you and your character.

2. <u>The choices I make can determine victory or defeat in my fight.</u>

Aside from Jesus, two thieves were also in the fight of their lives while hanging on the cross (Lk. 23:39-43). Although they were in the same situation, their outcomes were different because they made different decisions. One thief decided to mock Jesus. The other thief met Jesus and said, "Lord, remember me when you come into your kingdom." The thief who mocked Jesus died and went to hell, eternally separated from Jesus. The thief who met Jesus died and went to Heaven to be with Jesus eternally.

This tells us that two people can be in the same fight but have different outcomes according to the decisions that they make. There are other people who've already been defeated by the fight that you are currently in. There is no need to fear. Although they were defeated, you can have victory if you make different spiritual, mental, emotional, and sometimes even physical decisions. I pray that God grants you his wisdom to make the right decisions that please him at all times so that you can win your fight. Wisdom does not have to come from experience. It can come simply by asking God for it (1Kg. 3:1-15, Jms.1:5). Today's decisions determine tomorrow's victories or tomorrow's defeats.

3. <u>God can give me strength to help others in the midst of my own fight.</u>
When Jesus was in the fight of his life, hanging on a cross, one thief asked for help. The thief said, "Lord, remember me when you come into your kingdom" (Lk. 23:39-43). One of the hardest things is to entertain the thought of helping others when you are in middle of your own fight. Yet, this is exactly what Jesus did. Jesus didn't just entertain the thought of helping others. He actually did it. Jesus responded by saying, "Today, you will be with me in paradise" (Lk. 23:39-43).

The natural human tendency, while in the fight of our lives, is selfishness. We don't think about others. Even if we do think of others, we don't think we have the strength to help them. However, God can give us supernatural strength to help others, even in the middle of our own fights.

It wasn't enough for Jesus to go from pain to paradise. He took someone with him. When we stop trying to prove ourselves, make wise decisions that please God, and think of others, God moves us from pain to paradise. Remember that paradise is not just for you. It's meant for others as well. It's possible to be in paradise and still be lonely if we don't reach out to others and bring them along with us. It's painful right now, but don't give up. Paradise is just around the corner. God has an eternal paradise prepared for you in Heaven. There is also paradise on Earth, a place of peace that surpasses our circumstances that can only be experienced in close relationship with God.

It's Time to Throw Hands

- Am I trying to prove myself unnecessarily in this fight?
- What choices do I need to make to win this fight?
- Who can I help, while fighting my own fight?

-Prayer:

Lord, help me to reframe from trying to prove myself. May my service to you and work for you speak loudly on my behalf. Give me wisdom to make the right decisions. Give me strength to help others, even when I feel as if I'm at my wits end, in Jesus name, AMEN!

CHAPTER 10
Finish

As painful as things were, Jesus finished his fight on the cross (Jn. 19:30). He didn't quit. He didn't stop. He didn't give up. Paul followed the example of Jesus. Paul was in ministry, yet he experienced the fight of his life. When he came to the end, he recorded these words:

For I am now ready to be offered, and the time of my departure is at hand. I have fought a good fight, I have finished my course, I have kept the faith: There is henceforth laid up for me a crown of righteousness, which the Lord, the righteous judge, shall give me at that day: and not to me only, but unto all them also that love his appearing. Do your diligence to come shortly to me. For Demas has forsaken me, having loved this present world, and is departed unto

Thessalonica; Crescens to Galatia, Titus unto Dalmatia. Only Luke is with me. Take Mark, and bring him with you: for he is profitable to me for ministry......Alexander the coppersmith did me much evil: the Lord reward him according to his works: of whom beware, for he greatly withstood our words. At my first answer no man stood with me, but all men forsook me: I pray God that it may not be laid to their charge. Notwithstanding the Lord stood with me, and strengthened me; that by me the preaching might be fully known, and that all the Gentiles might hear: and I was delivered out of the mouth of the lion. And the Lord shall deliver me from every evil work, and will preserve me unto his heavenly kingdom: to whom be glory forever and ever. Amen (2Tim. 4:6-18).

While on death row and facing the fight of his life in a prison cell, Paul wrote to Timothy. Paul was exiting the scene stage left, and Timothy was entering the scene stage right. Paul was literally passing the baton of ministry to Timothy so that Paul's ministry didn't die with him. Ministry should be about the message, mission, and the man named Jesus, not about the individual man who preaches the message. When we put the message, mission, and man Jesus over the man who preaches the gospel, it keeps the ministry from being personality-driven. As a result, the ministry continues even in the absence of the one who preaches. As Paul wrote to Timothy, he told him of several fights that he experienced during his ministry and how he finished despite much adversity. From this, we learn a few things about finishing.

1. <u>Finishing requires us to put eternal joy over temporary pain.</u>

Before Paul died, he shared his wisdom with Timothy. After telling Timothy that "I've fought a good fight," Paul then said, "There is laid up for me a crown of righteousness, which the Lord, the righteous judge, shall give me at that day: and not to me only, but unto all them also that love his appearing." In his present fight, Paul was facing death. At the same time, Paul wasn't focused on obtaining the temporary satisfaction of freedom. He was focused on his eternal reward: the crown of righteousness. The crown of righteousness is not only for the giants of the faith like Paul. It's for all who love the appearing of Jesus Christ. The bottom line is this: when we live life in focus of eternity's joy, our temporary pains do not compare. Knowing this brings present joy and helps us through our current fight.

Jesus modeled the same example. After the Hebrew writer talked about laying aside every weight and running the race of life with patience, the writer then said, "Looking unto Jesus the author and finisher of our faith; who for the joy that was set before him endured the cross, despising the shame, and is set down at the right hand of the throne of God" (Heb. 12:2). When Jesus was in the fight of his life on the cross, his focus was eternal joy over temporary pain. His eternal joy was knowing that his fight was not in vain. His victory would save all who believe in him, reunite them with their Heavenly Father, and allow them to spend eternity in Heaven. I'm sure that the thought of this during his fight is what helped him make it through his fight.

When we find ourselves in the fight of our life, we must finish. Sometimes, winning is not finishing in a certain time length. Sometimes, winning is just finishing at all. Finishing requires us to live life in focus of eternity and to place future joy over temporary pain. This can only be done when we know that our fight means something. Your fight is not in vain. It means something. It is your current victory that will help others in the future.

2. <u>Finishing requires us to thank God for the people who left us that we wanted to stay with us.</u>

When speaking to Timothy, Paul mentioned, "Demas has forsaken me, having loved this present world, and is departed unto Thessalonica; Crescens to Galatia, Titus unto Dalmatia" (2Tim. 4:10). After being a co-laborer of the gospel with Paul for years, Demas deserted Paul. He left Paul because he valued the things of the world over the current mission of the gospel. By the way that Paul states this, he seems to condemn Demas for leaving. Paul mentions other people who left but not for the same reasons. I'm sure that Paul was hurt by Demas leaving.

When we are in the fight of our lives, we will experience people who leave us that we wished would have stayed with us. It is in these moments when we don't understand that we must thank God. If someone is with you in body, but their mind and heart are both somewhere else, they are not really with you at all. Remember, you don't just need people that you can count. Rather, you need people that you can count on.

3. <u>Finishing requires us to thank God for the people who stayed with us that we needed.</u>

After mentioning, "Demas has forsaken me," Paul then said, "Only Luke is with me" (2Tim. 4:11). God allowed Demas to leave, but he allowed Luke to stay. Luke was a physician—perhaps exactly what Paul needed during his stay in prison. It is very likely that Paul was suffering physically. Despite his suffering, God left a physician with him.

When we find ourselves in the fight of our lives, God always provides what we need and who we need. God loves us so much. He loves us too much to let us go through the fight of our lives alone. God is very strategic in whom he allows to leave, and he is very strategic in whom he allows to stay. Knowing this helps us trust the providence and sovereignty of God. Even when we can't see it, God is in control. Thank God for the people who stayed with you in the fight of your life.

4. <u>Finishing requires us to reconcile when necessary.</u>

Just before he died, Paul specifically asked Timothy to bring John-Mark (2Tim. 4:11). After Paul's first missionary journey with Barnabas and John-Mark, he parted ways with both of them (Acts 15:38-40). Paul's disagreement was with Barnabas, but it was because of John-Mark. John-Mark deserted Paul and Barnabas on the first missionary journey. Paul did not deem John-Mark worthy of going on the second missionary journey. Paul and Barnabas disagreed on this matter, which led to them parting ways.

At the end of Paul's life, Paul asked Timothy to bring John-Mark (2Tim. 4:11). The fact that Paul did this helps us to see that Paul was open to reconciliation. It also helps us to see that those who were not profitable to us in the past could still be profitable to us in the present and future.

The point of the matter is this: we can't win the fight of our lives with bitterness and unforgiveness lurking in our hearts. We must always remain open for reconciliation. At the same time, true reconciliation can only take place where there is true repentance. Forgiveness takes place, even without repentance. However, reconciliation can only take place with repentance. Both parties must examine themselves, turn from their ways, and turn to God. As two people draw closer to God, they draw closer to one another.

5. <u>Finishing requires us to thank God for the people who stayed with us that we wish would have left us.</u>

After mentioning several people, Paul then said, "Alexander the coppersmith did me much evil: the Lord reward him according to his works:" (2Tim. 4:14). Paul never said exactly what Alexander the coppersmith did to him. The only thing that we know is that Alexander acted in an evil way.

What do you do when the people you wanted to stay end up leaving, and the people you wanted to leave end up staying? It's one thing for people not to help you. It's another thing for people to work against you and cause you harm. This is exactly what Paul experienced. Even if Paul wanted to retaliate, he refused. He left Alexander in the hands of the Lord. We must do the same thing. To retaliate is to show in our actions that we don't trust him to take care of the situation. Even when it looks as if people are getting away with murder, they are not. God sees all, and he knows all. He loves you more than you know, and he will take vengeance. It's the people who stay that we wish would leave who keep us on our knees and drive us closer to God. We must thank God, even for these people.

6. <u>Finishing requires us to realize that God is with us.</u>

When Paul was on trial and no one stood with him, the Lord stood with him (2Tim. 4:16-18). The presence of God both strengthened and delivered Paul. Because of this, Paul was able to continue preaching the gospel in the face of adversity. He also had confidence in God's deliverance and that God would preserve him for the heavenly kingdom.

Though you may be in the fight of your life, God is with you. He's not sitting by passively. God is actively with you. God is strengthening you, and he is certainly both willing and able to deliver you on this side of Heaven. However, if God chooses a different path for us out of his sovereignty, may our commitment to God be so strong that we do not waver. We don't just win the fight of our lives when our circumstance changes. We win the fight of our lives when we have an unwavering commitment to God in spite of our circumstance. Because of Jesus Christ living inside of you, you are a winner. Victory is already yours.

It's Time to Throw Hands

- What pains me at this moment?
- Who in my life has left me that I wish would have stayed?
- Who is with me that I need at this moment?
- Who should I reconcile with?
- Who is with me that I wish would leave?

-Prayer:

Lord give me strength to finish this fight strong in a way that pleases you. Some have left that I wish would have stayed; however, thank you for those who are with me to help at this moment. Show me whom I should reconcile with and whom I should stay away from, in Jesus' name, AMEN!

Conclusion:
A PRAYER FOR VICTORY

Father, in the mighty name of Jesus Christ, I thank you for the person who has read this book. Perhaps they read it when going through their own personal pain. Perhaps they read it with tears in their eyes. Perhaps they read it with past and present hurts. Maybe they even read it in preparation for a future fight. Regardless of when or why they read this book, I thank you for them.

Lord, I pray that the words of this book would penetrate their ears and flow into the depths of their hearts. Open their ears to hear you speak to them. Open their eyes to see you through the conveyed truths of this book. Open their hearts to receive you and your help for the fight of their lives. Open their minds and grant them understanding. Give them supernatural wisdom that only you can give, that they may know how to apply what they have learned.

I thank you, Jesus, that the person who has read this book is more than a conqueror (Rom. 8:37). I thank you that no weapon formed against him/her shall be able to prosper (Isa. 54:17). I thank you in advance for the victory through our Lord and Savior, Jesus the Christ (1Cor. 15:58). I plead the blood of Jesus over this reader's mind, heart, body, soul, and spirit. I thank you that just as the death angel passed over the Israelites (your children) because of your blood on the doorpost (Ex. 12), every demonic spirit, thought, and generational curse of, sickness, death, disease, poverty, bitterness, unforgiveness, rejection, rebellion, confusion, disorder, chaos, anger, wrath, malice, hatred, resentment, envy, jealousy, pride, arrogance, divorce, separation, infidelity, masturbation, lust, pornography, sexual immorality, sexual perversion, adultery, fornication, physical abuse, emotional abuse, mental abuse, spiritual abuse, sexual abuse, financial abuse, psychological abuse, and domestic violence, is passing over us because of your blood that covers us.

You were wounded for our transgressions. You were bruised for our iniquities. The chastisement of our peace was upon your shoulders, and by your stripes we are healed (Isa. 53:5). We thank you for these and many other victories in the mighty and matchless name of you our Lord and Savior, Jesus the Christ, who's able to do absolutely anything but fail, Hallelujah, thank you Jesus, and Amen.

www.ingramcontent.com/pod-product-compliance
Lightning Source LLC
Chambersburg PA
CBHW070501090426
42735CB00012B/2645